THE PREDICTIONS LIBRARY

PALMISTRY

David V. Barrett

A DORLING KINDERSLEY BOOK

Senior Editor • Sharon Lucas
Art Editor • Anna Benjamin
Managing Editor • Krystyna Mayer
Managing Art Editor • Derek Coombes
DTP Designer • Cressida Joyce
Production Controller • Sarah Fuller
US Editor • Connie Mersel

First American Edition, 1995
2 4 6 8 10 9 7 5 3

Published in the United States by DK Publishing, Inc.,
95 Madison Avenue, New York, New York 10016
Copyright © 1995 Dorling Kindersley Limited, London
Visit us on the World Wide Web at
http://www.dk.com

Distributed by Houghton Mifflin Company, Boston.

Library of Congress Cataloging-in-Publication Data

Barrett, David V.
    Palmistry / by David V. Barrett. -- 1st American ed.
        p.   cm. -- (The predictions library)
    ISBN 0-7894-0311-0
    1. Palmistry.   I. Title.   II. Series: Barrett, David V.
Predictions library.
BF921.B28   1995
133.8--dc20
                                                            95-11682
                                                                CIP

Reproduced by Bright Arts, Hong Kong
Printed and bound in Hong Kong by Imago

CONTENTS

INTRODUCING
PALMISTRY

YOUR HANDS CONTAIN THE STORY OF YOUR LIFE. THE
PALMS CAN SHOW SURPRISINGLY ACCURATE
INFORMATION ABOUT YOURSELF, SUCH AS YOUR
UPBRINGING, STRENGTHS, AND WEAKNESSES.

Palm readers examine the whole hand, including the back, the fingers, and the fingertips. Fingerprints were first studied and classified by the British anthropologist Francis Galton (1822–1911). They are now an essential part of police work, and could be seen as a practical application of palmistry.

~ ⊙ ~

Every person's palms are unique; no two palms are exactly the same. According to palm readers, the shape, texture, color, and especially, the lines on a palm are a blueprint or map of their owner's life.

~ ⊙ ~

It is traditional for palm readers to tell you your future, including how many

MAGIC PALMISTRY
Palm reading has often been considered occult, but modern palmists treat it in a far more scientific manner than this early 20th-century French manual.

children you will have, and how wealthy you will be. Reading the future in your hands is called chiromancy. Many palm readers, however, concentrate more on reading your character, which is known as chirognomy.

～❦～

In the past, and in non-Western cultures, it has usually been believed that your hands also show the state of your health. In recent years, some Western doctors have begun to accept that certain medical conditions can be revealed in the palms of your hands, which lends weight to the claims of palm readers that your life is revealed in your hands.

～❦～

It is not widely known that the lines on your palms, including the major lines, change over the months and years. Minor lines appear and disappear, become stronger, or fade altogether. Breaks occur or are mended. During your life, your personality develops, and your health improves or deteriorates; the lines on your hands change to reflect

MEASURING UP
For centuries, various parts of the body have been analyzed. This 1886 illustration shows a phrenological examination. Phrenology assessed your character from your skull's size and shape, and every bump or hollow was measured for its significance.

these developments. As with all forms of divination, palmistry does not foretell a fixed future. Your hands can show traits, indications, and possibilities, but it is always up to you to take what life has given you and make of it what you can.

HISTORY
of PALMISTRY

OVER THE CENTURIES, PALMISTRY'S REPUTATION HAS FLUCTUATED CONSIDERABLY BETWEEN SERIOUS ACADEMIC STUDY AND SENSATIONALIZED SUPERSTITIOUS NONSENSE.

Palmistry is thousands of years old. It may have originated in India or China, and it is mentioned in the Hindu scriptures and the Old Testament. It was practiced in the ancient countries of the Middle East, and by the Classical Greeks and Romans. The Christian Church condemned palm reading, but this had little effect on its practice.

~ ☉ ~

During the Crusades (1096–1291), Western intellectuals, including scholars of the esoteric arts, were greatly influenced by medieval Arab thought, which was itself partly a distillation of ancient Egyptian beliefs. During the 16th and 17th centuries in Western Europe, Hermetic philosophers, doctors, theologians, astrologers, and alchemists added the art of

CHEIRO'S CHAIR
This portrait of Cheiro dates from 1895. Although he popularized palmistry in the 19th century, he did not add to its reputation.

MEANINGS OF THE MARKS
This 15th-century illustration shows how the marks
on your palm affect your fate. For example, the man
on the right of the gallows is holding his arms up in
dismay. He has a cross, which represents ill fortune,
and a star, which represents a frightening event.

reading palms to their skills. The Romanies, or gypsies, also spread the fascination with fortune-telling from the hand, as well as Tarot and tea-leaf reading.

In the 19th century, the fairground type of fortune-telling by palm readers continued. The most famous palm reader of all, Count Louis Hamon, or Cheiro (*c.* 1860–1936), was reputed to be astonishingly accurate, and was said to have foretold the love affair and abdication of King Edward VIII five years before the event. Many serious scientific studies were also made during this time by French scholars and doctors. These works formed the basis for later studies by psychologists in Europe and America in the 20th century. Many contemporary palm readers consider their work to be a science that follows clear and well-validated rules, but the fortune-telling aspect of palmistry still remains.

RIGHT & LEFT
HANDS

A GOOD PALMIST WILL READ BOTH HANDS. THIS WILL
SHOW THE SORT OF PERSON YOU ARE NOW, WHERE YOU
HAVE COME FROM IN YOUR LIFE, AND HOW YOUR
CHARACTER HAS DEVELOPED.

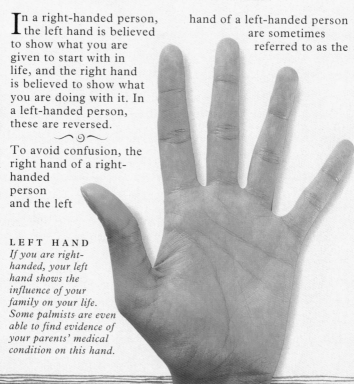

In a right-handed person, the left hand is believed to show what you are given to start with in life, and the right hand is believed to show what you are doing with it. In a left-handed person, these are reversed.

~ ∾ ~

To avoid confusion, the right hand of a right-handed person and the left

hand of a left-handed person are sometimes referred to as the

LEFT HAND
If you are right-handed, your left hand shows the influence of your family on your life. Some palmists are even able to find evidence of your parents' medical condition on this hand.

dominant or active hand, and the other hand is called the passive hand.

~ ❧ ~

When a palmist looks for deep-seated family influences, these will normally be found on the passive hand. The lines on your dominant hand show how you have developed in the light of these early influences. Other palmists, however, prefer to see the passive hand as showing what you are secretly like, deep inside, and the dominant hand as the external personality that you project to the world.

~ ❧ ~

A careful comparison of your right and left hands can show whether you have made use of inherent abilities, or whether you are wasting them. The comparison might also reveal if you are over-compensating for a naturally shy personality by presenting yourself as lively and confident, or instead, whether the lack of confidence that you may often feel in yourself is in any way justified or not.

RIGHT HAND
If you are right-handed, your right hand is more likely to show events that have happened to you, such as a serious illness or the traumatic breakup of a relationship. It also shows what you are making of your life.

POSITION & COLOR

A PALMIST STARTS TO FORM AN IMPRESSION OF YOUR
PERSONALITY BEFORE EXAMINING THE LINES ON YOUR
PALM. THIS IMPRESSION IS CREATED BY OBSERVING THE
POSITION IN WHICH YOU HOLD YOUR HANDS, AND
THEIR TEXTURE AND COLOR.

In everyday speech, it is common to refer to people as being "tight-fisted" or "open-handed." Shaking hands with someone can be very revealing – for example, does the hand have a firm or gentle grip, is it loose and floppy, or is the palm dry or sweaty? Palmists look for similar physical characteristics when they first examine your hands.

Some palmists may ask you to grip their fingers as hard as you can. This helps them judge your physical strength and, to some extent, your strength of will. They will also, during the reading, manipulate your hand.

HAND COLOR
The color of your hands can indicate the state of your health. Very pale hands such as this one might be revealing a tendency towards anemia. A very red palm can indicate high blood pressure or diabetes. Bluish skin can indicate poor circulation, unless the hands are simply cold. A normal, healthy palm is pink in color.

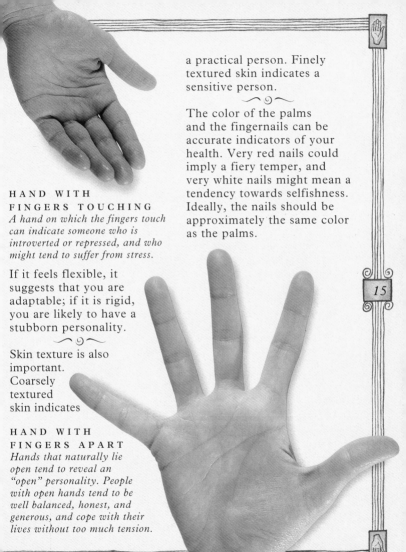

a practical person. Finely textured skin indicates a sensitive person.

The color of the palms and the fingernails can be accurate indicators of your health. Very red nails could imply a fiery temper, and very white nails might mean a tendency towards selfishness. Ideally, the nails should be approximately the same color as the palms.

HAND WITH FINGERS TOUCHING
A hand on which the fingers touch can indicate someone who is introverted or repressed, and who might tend to suffer from stress.

If it feels flexible, it suggests that you are adaptable; if it is rigid, you are likely to have a stubborn personality.

Skin texture is also important. Coarsely textured skin indicates

HAND WITH FINGERS APART
Hands that naturally lie open tend to reveal an "open" personality. People with open hands tend to be well balanced, honest, and generous, and cope with their lives without too much tension.

TRADITIONAL
HAND SHAPES

MANY PALMISTS STILL USE THE TRADITIONAL
CLASSIFICATION OF SEVEN TYPES OF HAND SHAPE AS
A STARTING POINT TO HELP THEM DISTINGUISH
BETWEEN BASIC TYPES OF CHARACTER.

ELEMENTARY

SQUARE

PSYCHIC

The seven traditional hand shapes – elementary, square, psychic, conic, philosophic, spatulate, and mixed – were proposed by the French palmist Casimir d'Arpentigny in the 19th century. The characteristics associated with the hand shapes reflect 19th-century sociological ideas.

~ୄ~

The elementary hand is stubby and sturdy. It has a square palm and short fingers, and looks coarse. There are usually few lines; these are often deeply cut. This hand indicates a steady but predictable person. In 19th-century terms, this could be the hand of an unskilled manual worker.

~ୄ~

The palm of the square hand is as broad as it is long, and the fingers are straight and square-tipped. A square-handed person is likely to be practical, systematic, and

CONIC   PHILO-   SPATULATE   MIXED
SOPHIC

suited to skilled manual work, but could also be a good bureaucrat or engineer.

The psychic hand is an elongated version of the conic hand, with pointed fingertips. Psychic-handed people tend to be intuitive, spiritual, and oversensitive.

The conic hand is fairly common among women. The base of the palm and the fingertips tend to be slightly tapered, and the skin is finely textured. This hand suggests sensitivity and creativity.

The philosophic hand is long, with bony fingers and large, "knotted" knuckles. This hand denotes a deep thinker. Although the knotty fingers

are the distinguishing characteristic, they can appear in any hand shape.

The spatulate hand has bulbous fingertips, especially on the middle fingers. People with spatulate hands tend to be energetic, active, creative, and practical. They can be good athletes, or innovators in any career.

The mixed hand contains a mixture of the other types of hand shape. The palm might suggest one type of hand, but the fingers might suggest another. Mixed-handed people are likely to have a combination of the qualities of the other hand types. Consequently they are multitalented and adaptable.

ELEMENTAL
HAND SHAPES

MANY MODERN PALMISTS PREFER TO USE A NEW
CLASSIFICATION OF HAND TYPES, BASED ON THE FOUR
ANCIENT AND ESOTERIC ELEMENTS OF EARTH, AIR,
FIRE, AND WATER.

EARTH

The Earth hand has square palms and short fingers. It is similar to the traditional square hand. Earth hands usually have few lines; these are deeply cut. Earth-handed people tend to be practical, "earthy," and materialistic. They are reliable and strong in character. They tend to be unadventurous and possibly stubborn. They like routine, order, and security.

AIR

The air hand has square palms and long fingers. It is similar to the traditional conic hand. Air-handed people are intelligent, and excellent communicators. They have an investigative

nature and want to acquire more knowledge. Their temperament can be changeable, and they are often impatient with other people's slow thinking. They tend to be ruled by their mind, and can find it difficult to reveal their emotions.

FIRE

The fire hand has rectangular palms and short fingers. It is similar to the traditional spatulate hand. Fire-handed people are energetic, restless, and ambitious. They are intelligent, and very lively and sociable. Although they are good organizers, sometimes they are too impulsive to be reliable, and may appear to be aggressive. They tend to throw all their resources into whatever they are doing at the present time, and may "burn out" in the process.

EARTH HAND

AIR HAND

FIRE HAND

WATER HAND

WATER

The water hand has rectangular palms and long fingers. It is similar to the traditional psychic hand. It can often be recognized by the many fine lines all over the palm.

Water-handed people are very intuitive. They are highly sensitive, both in sensing other people's feelings, and in being easily hurt themselves. They are intelligent and creative, but have a tendency to be introverted. Quiet and thoughtful, they can easily become lost in their dreams and fantasies.

THE NAILS

THE SHAPE OF THE NAILS, LIKE THE SHAPE OF THE HANDS, CAN SUGGEST DIFFERENT CHARACTER TYPES. IN ADDITION, THE NAILS CAN BE EXAMINED IN ORDER TO GAUGE YOUR LEVEL OF HEALTH, NUTRITION, AND TENDENCY TOWARDS STRESS.

ALMOND   LONG ALMOND   CLAWLIKE

Ideally, the nails should be in proportion to the fingers in length and breadth. The nails should be slightly longer than they are wide, and curved across the fingertip and along their length.

～ ๑ ～

The nails are usually classified according to their overall size, and whether they are wide or narrow, long or short. The length of the nail refers only to the pink and living part; the white, dead, and trimmable part can be ignored.

～ ๑ ～

Almond-shaped nails, rounded at each end, are differentiated by their width. A wide but well-proportioned almond nail can indicate a happy nature, a romantic disposition, and a tendency to avoid confrontation. Long, almond nails might show an intuitive person who is also

| BROAD | VERY NARROW | SQUARE AND SHORT | SQUARE |

likely to be overly nervous. Clawlike nails can suggest someone with a passionate, even violent, emotional life.

Large, broad nails can indicate a quick temper, and small, broad nails often show someone who is intolerant and critical of others. A fan-shaped nail, wider at the end than at its base, often denotes someone who is emotionally high-strung. Long, narrow nails suggest a kind and sensitive person, but very narrow nails can indicate a neurotic individual. Square and short nails indicate a narrow and stubborn nature, and square nails, particularly those with a square base, usually show a stable and practical character.

Deep ridges across the nails can indicate nutritional problems or severe nervous shock. Ridges along the nails' length show nervous tension, but they can also indicate rheumatism or a hyperactive thyroid. Brittle nails can show an underactive thyroid. Soft nails usually show a dietary deficiency, such as a lack of calcium or protein.

Preferably, the nails should be the same color as the palms. Very red nails might reveal a hot temper, but also high blood pressure. (For other health indicators from nail color, see *Health, page 45*.) If health problems are shown in the nails, the indications should disappear when good health is restored.

THE FINGERS & THUMB

THE FINGERS AND THUMB ARE GOOD INDICATORS OF
YOUR CHARACTER. PALMISTS EXAMINE YOUR FINGERS
AND THUMB TO DISCOVER THE AREAS OF LIFE IN WHICH
YOU ARE MOST OR LEAST PROFICIENT.

SQUARE   POINTED   CONIC   SPATULATE

Each of the fingers is named after one of the planets or gods – the index finger (Jupiter), the middle finger (Saturn), the third or ring finger (Apollo), and the little finger (Mercury). The thumb corresponds to Venus.

All the fingers are associated with certain attributes, and the longer the finger, the stronger these attributes. The index finger represents ambition and leadership, and the middle finger is linked with justice and morality. The ring finger is connected to the subconscious and creativity, and the little finger represents communication and self-expression.

There are four basic types of finger shape – square, pointed, conic, and spatulate. Square fingers suggest good sense and conventionality, and pointed fingers can reveal sensitivity and an impractical nature. Conic fingers denote spontaneity and inconsistency, and spatulate fingers may indicate enthusiasm and an enterprising spirit.

~ 9 ~

The thumb represents strength of character. A large thumb can reveal a domineering nature, and a short thumb can indicate a lack of will power. A firm-jointed thumb suggests resilience and inflexibility, and a loose-jointed thumb denotes a broad, honest mind, and impulsiveness.

~ 9 ~

The phalanges are the joints of the fingers. The top phalange, with the fingernail, represents the mental, the middle phalange is linked to the practical, and the lowest phalange is connected with the materialistic. The thumb's top phalange represents willpower, and its lower phalange denotes reasoning ability. If a phalange is markedly longer or shorter than the other phalanges on the finger, it reveals an emphasis on the specific area of abilities.

FIRM-JOINTED THUMB

~ 9 ~

LOOSE-JOINTED THUMB

THE MOUNTS

THE QUALITIES OF THE FINGERS ARE MOST IMPORTANT
IN RELATION TO THE FLESHY MOUNDS ON THE PALM,
KNOWN AS MOUNTS, AT THE BASE OF EACH FINGER.
THESE MOUNTS ALSO GIVE SIGNIFICANCE TO WHERE
THE LINES LIE ON THE PALM.

The mount of Venus is the large, fleshy pad that is the enclosed bottom joint of the thumb. It indicates the value that you place on love, sensuality, and beauty.

The mount of Jupiter lies below the index finger. It reveals your leadership qualities, personal pride, and material success in life. An overdeveloped mount of Jupiter can reveal an unhealthy love of power.

The mount of Saturn lies below the middle finger. It represents seriousness and responsibility. The mount of Apollo lies below the ring finger. It relates to creativity, the arts, and your level of contentment with life. The mount of Mercury lies below the little finger. It reveals

your communication skills, and how you respond to excitement and change.

The fleshiness on the lower percussive edge of the palm, opposite the mount of Venus, is the mount of Luna. It is linked with the subconscious. If it is highly developed it can reveal excessive romanticism.

Some mounts, such as the mounts of Jupiter and Mars, are notoriously difficult to find. The mount of Neptune is an area that lies between the mounts of Luna and Venus. The mount of Mars active lies between the thumb base and the index finger base, and the mount of Mars passive lies between the middle of the percussive side, between the mounts of Mercury and Luna.

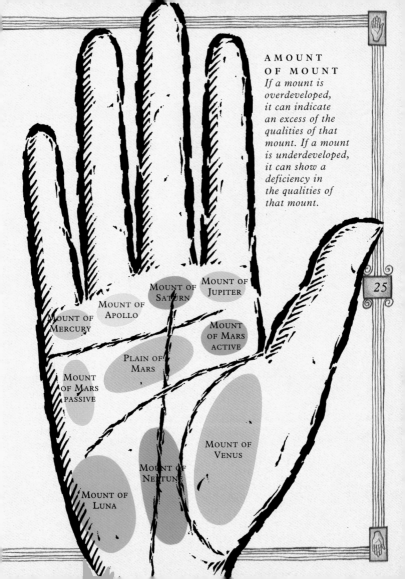

AMOUNT OF MOUNT
If a mount is overdeveloped, it can indicate an excess of the qualities of that mount. If a mount is underdeveloped, it can show a deficiency in the qualities of that mount.

MOUNT OF JUPITER

MOUNT OF SATURN

MOUNT OF APOLLO

MOUNT OF MERCURY

MOUNT OF MARS ACTIVE

PLAIN OF MARS

MOUNT OF MARS PASSIVE

MOUNT OF VENUS

MOUNT OF NEPTUNE

MOUNT OF LUNA

THE AREAS
of THE PALM

DIFFERENT AREAS OF THE PALM REPRESENT VARIOUS
APPROACHES TO LIFE, REVEALING THE BALANCE
BETWEEN YOUR RATIONAL, INTELLECTUAL SIDE, AND
YOUR INSTINCTIVE, INTUITIVE SIDE.

Some palmists divide the palm into four zones. First, a vertical line is drawn halfway across the palm. The percussive side shows the unconscious or instinctive aspects of your character, and the thumb side represents your conscious, rational, or logical aspects. Next, a horizontal line, drawn just above the joining of thumb and palm, divides the palm into an upper, mental zone, and a lower, physical zone.

~ ی ~

Other palmists divide the palm into nine zones. First, three vertical bands are formed by drawing lines down from either side of the middle finger. Below the little finger and ring finger lies the passive, subconscious zone, and below the index finger

and thumb lies the active, conscious zone, with a zone of balance in between. Next, three horizontal bands are drawn, which separate the mounts. The upper zone is the emotional, conscious zone, and includes the four finger mounts. The bottom zone is the instinctive, unconscious zone, and includes the mounts of Luna and Venus. Between these two zones is a zone of balance, which contains the two mounts and the plain of Mars.

~ ی ~

Whichever way the palm is divided, the bottom corner on the percussive side of the palm is always related to the subconscious, and the top corner immediately below the index finger is always related to the conscious.

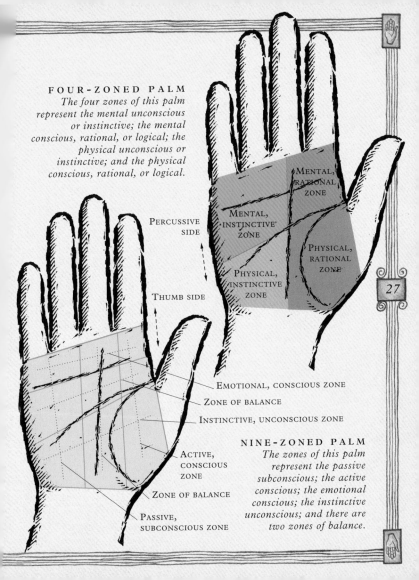

FOUR-ZONED PALM
The four zones of this palm represent the mental unconscious or instinctive; the mental conscious, rational, or logical; the physical unconscious or instinctive; and the physical conscious, rational, or logical.

MENTAL, RATIONAL ZONE

MENTAL, INSTINCTIVE ZONE

PHYSICAL, RATIONAL ZONE

PHYSICAL, INSTINCTIVE ZONE

PERCUSSIVE SIDE

THUMB SIDE

27

EMOTIONAL, CONSCIOUS ZONE

ZONE OF BALANCE

INSTINCTIVE, UNCONSCIOUS ZONE

ACTIVE, CONSCIOUS ZONE

ZONE OF BALANCE

PASSIVE, SUBCONSCIOUS ZONE

NINE-ZONED PALM
The zones of this palm represent the passive subconscious; the active conscious; the emotional conscious; the instinctive unconscious; and there are two zones of balance.

THE LIFE LINE

THE LIFE LINE IS THE CURVED LINE AROUND THE
PADDED AREA AT THE THUMB'S BASE. THE CURVE,
DIRECTION, DEPTH, AND ANY BREAKS OR MARKINGS ON
THE LIFE LINE ARE MORE IMPORTANT THAN ITS LENGTH.

There is a common misconception that your Life line shows the length of your life, and that a short Life line, or one which is broken, means an early death. This is totally incorrect. The Life line shows the vitality of your life rather than its length.

The depth and clarity of the Life line is important. A deep, firm line holds fewer problems than a line that is weak and wavery. This applies both to health and to

your ability to cope with the normal pressures of life. A strong, deep line is likely to show that you are a fighter against disease, and a weak line suggests a greater

TIGHT CURVE
A tightly curved Life line that lies close in to the thumb suggests constriction and inhibition. If the mount of Venus is also small, it can indicate a self-absorbed personality.

LIFE LINE
IS TIGHTLY
CURVED AND
LIES CLOSE IN
TO THUMB

MOUNT
OF VENUS
IS SMALL

susceptibility to illnesses. A deep, red Life line shows this fighting characteristic moving into aggression.

The Life line starts midway between the index finger and the thumb, and is often joined to the Head line at the beginning. The point at which these two lines separate is supposed to indicate when you achieved independence from your childhood home. A complete or very early separation of the two lines indicates that you were highly independent even as a child.

Sometimes there is a fainter "shadow" Life line, which signifies added protection. A Life line that swings out towards the mount of Luna shows a restless nature. The Life line can also record your health, with islands and breaks on the line showing weak periods and disruptive breaks in your life.

LIFE LINE IS WIDELY CURVED AROUND THE MOUNT OF VENUS

WIDE CURVE
A widely curving Life line suggests a warm, outgoing personality. This person is likely to enjoy the sensual side of life. The Life line goes around the mount of Venus, which is indicative of emotions and sexuality.

MOUNT OF LUNA

THE HEART LINE

THE HEART LINE IS THE UPPER LINE OF THE TWO
ROUGHLY HORIZONTAL LINES IN THE TOP PART OF THE
PALM. THE HEART LINE GIVES AN INDICATION OF BOTH
THE EMOTIONAL HEART AND THE PHYSICAL HEART.

A s with all the lines, the depth and firmness of the Heart line are important, as well as its position and direction. A strong line shows emotional confidence and security, and a weak line shows someone who, because of emotional insecurity, is likely to have difficulty forming relationships.

~ ⊙ ~

A wide gap between the Heart line and the base of the fingers signifies a generous and open-hearted person who is considerate and concerned about others. A Heart line very close to the fingers shows less concern for others, and thus perhaps a more selfish and calculating person. The distance between the Heart line and the Head line below it is

HEART
LINE
REACHES
BASE
OF
INDEX
FINGER

AFFAIRS OF THE HEART
A Heart line that ends on the mount of Apollo indicates an unrealistic idealist in matters of the heart. If your Heart line reaches the base of your index finger, it can show that you are loyal and possessive.

also important. A wide gap suggests an open-minded person, and a narrow gap suggests selfishness and a conventional nature.

~ ⊙ ~

The Heart line also reveals the sort of lover you are. A Heart line that curves upward shows a leaning towards a physical, earthy attitude to sex, and a straight Heart line shows someone for whom romance and sexual fantasies are important.

A curved Heart line can indicate someone who enjoys an active, dominant sexual role, and a straight Heart line might reveal someone who likes a more passive, receptive role.

~ ⊙ ~

Although it is unusual, sometimes the Heart line curves downward and crosses the Head and Life lines. This position is believed to reveal a deep emotional hurt in your past.

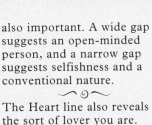

END OF THE LINE
If your Heart line ends between your middle and index fingers, it can show that although you are warm-hearted, you take a sensible, realistic attitude to your emotional relationships.

HEART LINE ENDS
BETWEEN MIDDLE
AND INDEX FINGERS

THE HEAD LINE
& SIMIAN LINE

THE HEAD LINE IS THE LOWER LINE OF THE TWO
APPROXIMATELY HORIZONTAL LINES IN THE UPPER
PART OF THE PALM. IT REVEALS YOUR INTELLIGENCE
AND YOUR APPROACH TO INTELLECTUAL PROBLEMS.

The Head line is often joined to the Life line at its start. If they remain joined for some distance, this may indicate a lack of self-confidence. If the two lines are widely separated from the very start, this can indicate too much self-confidence.

~∽~

A long Head line shows high intelligence, and intellectual breadth and flexibility.

A short Head line shows someone who thinks mainly about practical day-to-day matters. A strong Head line shows a person who is able

HEAD LINE CURVES
DOWNWARD

CURVED LINE
A Head line that curves downward is a strong indication of a creative and artistic temperament. Your approach to problem-solving is likely to be intuitive and instinctive rather than analytical. The longer the Head line and the steeper the curve, the less practical the person.

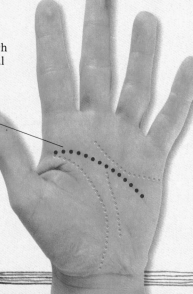

to concentrate and focus on whatever is being considered. A weak Head line indicates a lack of concentration and poor mental ability.

~ ☉ ~

A straight Head line shows an analytical way of thinking, and a curving line shows a more intuitive approach. These can point the way toward a career in either the sciences (a straight Head line) or the arts (a curved Head line). A fork at the end of the line is known as the Writer's Fork. As its name suggests, it can often show an ability for creative writing.

~ ☉ ~

Rarely, the Head line and the Heart line, coming from opposite sides

of the palm, join into one straight line. This is known as the Simian line. It shows that the heart and head are, literally, as one. Someone with a Simian line is likely to be extremely single-minded, intense, dogmatic, and will devote every part of themselves to whatever they choose to do.

HEAD LINE IS STRAIGHT

STRAIGHT LINE
A straight, almost horizontal Head line shows a rational, logical mind; you are likely to be practical rather than imaginative. A short Head line indicates a special focus on a small area, rather than a broad range of interests.

THE FATE LINE

THE FATE LINE USUALLY RUNS VERTICALLY UP THE
MIDDLE OF THE PALM, SOMETIMES FROM THE
RASCETTES, OR BRACELETS, ON THE WRIST TO THE
MOUNTS OF THE FINGERS. IT SHOWS HOW EXTERNAL
INFLUENCES MIGHT AFFECT YOUR LIFE.

Despite its name, the Fate line does not predetermine your fate or destiny, or foretell a fixed future. Your fate is always determined by you, and you are responsible for the course of your life. There are many external influences on your life, however, and some of these can have a major effect. The Fate line shows how likely you are to be affected by these influences.

Some people do not have a Fate line. Most palmists interpret this as an indication that you have control of your own destiny, or instead, that

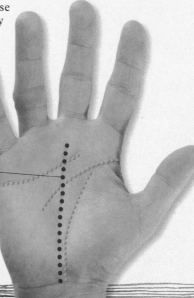

FATE LINE IS LONG, AND RUNS
FROM THE RASCETTES TO THE
HEAD AND HEART LINES

LONG FATE LINE
*This long Fate line runs
from the rascettes and up
through the Head and Heart
lines. It indicates an early
start in personal success, and
an urge to achieve.*

you follow where your life leads. The Fate line shows whether you are fulfilled or frustrated by your progress. It can be a measure of your success in terms of what you personally want to achieve.

~ 9 ~

The differences between the Fate lines in the passive and active hands (see *Right & Left Hands, pages 12–13*) can show how you have developed your potential. A strong Fate line reveals that you have control over your life, and a weak Fate line shows a lack of control.

~ 9 ~

A Fate line that begins on the Life line shows close family ties early in life. A Fate line ending on the mount of Jupiter indicates achieving a position of great influence. If the Fate line ends on the

Apollo, it shows success in the arts, and if it ends on the mount of Mercury it shows success in business. A Fate line that branches to more than one of the mounts is very favorable. Breaks in the Fate line show interruptions in your career, and if the parts of the line overlap, they point toward a smooth transition.

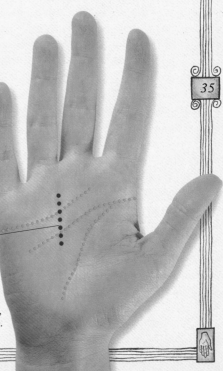

FATE LINE IS SHORT AND STARTS HIGH UP THE HAND

SHORT FATE LINE
The point on the palm where the Fate line begins reveals when you started becoming independent and making your own fate. This short Fate line starts high on the hand, and shows a late developer in life.

OTHER LINES

THERE ARE MANY OTHER LINES ON THE PALM THAT PROVIDE CONSIDERABLE DETAIL TO AN EXPERIENCED PALMIST. HOWEVER, THESE OTHER LINES ARE NOT PRESENT ON EVERY HAND, AND THEY CAN OFTEN BE DIFFICULT TO IDENTIFY.

The one, two, or three lines across the wrist at the base of the hand are known as the rascettes, or the bracelets. Traditionally they show fortune and good health, but a high loop in the top rascette of a woman can indicate possible gynecological problems.

The Girdle of Venus is a semicircular line found at the top of the palm, with one end between the index and middle fingers and the other end between the ring and little fingers. Although the Girdle of Venus denotes a passionate nature, it is not necessarily sexual. If you have a Girdle of Venus you might feel very strongly about certain

GIRDLE OF VENUS

APOLLO LINE
This line is also known as the Sun line, Success line, or Fame line. It is a vertical line that runs up to the ring finger, but it is often faint or not present. The Apollo line indicates acclaim and fulfillment.

APOLLO LINE

subjects, and be prone to extreme nervous tension and excitement.

~ⓞ~

The Marriage line, also known as the Relationship line, is on the percussive edge of the hand, just below the little finger. The number of lines used to be thought to correspond with how many times you might be married, but these lines are now thought to signify deep emotional relationships. Upward spurs tend to indicate emotional uplift and downward spurs can show problems.

~ⓞ~

The line or bow of Intuition lies on the mount of Luna, on the percussive side of the palm, and bows toward the center of the palm. This line is considered to be an indication of psychic awareness or ability. The deeper and clearer the line, the more intuitive or psychic you are likely to be. It is quite common for this line to be fragmented, if it is there at all.

HEALTH LINE
LINE OF INTUITION
RASCETTES

HEALTH LINE
This line is also known as the Mercury, Hepatic, or Liver line. It usually rises from the Life line or from either side of it and moves diagonally up the palm toward the little finger. It takes a skilled palmist to decide whether any particular version of this line refers to health, business, communication, or the arts.

OTHER MARKINGS
on THE PALM

AS WELL AS THE LENGTH, DEPTH, STRENGTH, AND
CONDITION OF EACH LINE, THERE ARE MANY OTHER
MARKINGS TO CONSIDER. THEY PROVIDE VALUABLE
INFORMATION TO THE EXPERIENCED PALMIST.

If a line becomes frayed, it points to a decrease in the power of the line. Fraying at the end of a line is likely to indicate the frailty of old age. A break in a line means an interruption. In the Fate and Career lines, this might mean a major change of job. However, in the Life line it might mean a traumatic event, such as a major illness or accident.

Forks at the end of a line are considered to be positive. A forked Head line suggests versatility, and a forked Heart line suggests a complex emotional makeup but

CHAINING
When part of a line looks like the links of a small chain, it signifies weakness or confusion. This is common at the beginning of the Life line, where it can show childhood illnesses. Chains on the Heart line can sometimes indicate circulatory trouble.

ISLANDS

CHAINING

BREAKS

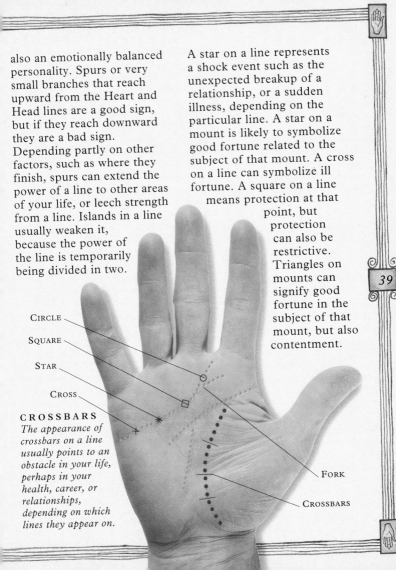

also an emotionally balanced personality. Spurs or very small branches that reach upward from the Heart and Head lines are a good sign, but if they reach downward they are a bad sign. Depending partly on other factors, such as where they finish, spurs can extend the power of a line to other areas of your life, or leech strength from a line. Islands in a line usually weaken it, because the power of the line is temporarily being divided in two.

A star on a line represents a shock event such as the unexpected breakup of a relationship, or a sudden illness, depending on the particular line. A star on a mount is likely to symbolize good fortune related to the subject of that mount. A cross on a line can symbolize ill fortune. A square on a line means protection at that point, but protection can also be restrictive. Triangles on mounts can signify good fortune in the subject of that mount, but also contentment.

CIRCLE

SQUARE

STAR

CROSS

CROSSBARS
The appearance of crossbars on a line usually points to an obstacle in your life, perhaps in your health, career, or relationships, depending on which lines they appear on.

FORK

CROSSBARS

RELATIONSHIPS

THE TEXTURE OF YOUR HAND, POSITIONING OF YOUR
FINGERS AND THUMB, PROMINENCE OF YOUR MOUNTS,
AND DETAILS OF THE LINES ON YOUR PALM ALL REVEAL
HOW WELL YOU CAN GET ALONG WITH OTHER PEOPLE
IN A CLOSE EMOTIONAL RELATIONSHIP.

A flexible hand reveals an easygoing personality, and a stiff hand suggests rigidity that might cause difficulty in relationships. The shape of the nails shows whether you are likely to be overly critical of the faults of others.

The angle that the thumb forms with the hand shows repression or inhibition; a close

angle suggests a puritanical attitude, and a wide angle shows open-mindedness. If the middle and ring fingers lie close together, it shows a need for the security of physical contact.

A well-developed mount of Venus reveals deep sensuality, but if it is too fleshy, it could

MARRIAGE LINE

HEART LINE
ENDS ON
INDEX FINGER,
INDICATING
NEED TO TAKE
LEAD IN
RELATIONSHIP

SMALL MOUNT
OF VENUS
SUGGESTS LACK
OF SENSUALITY

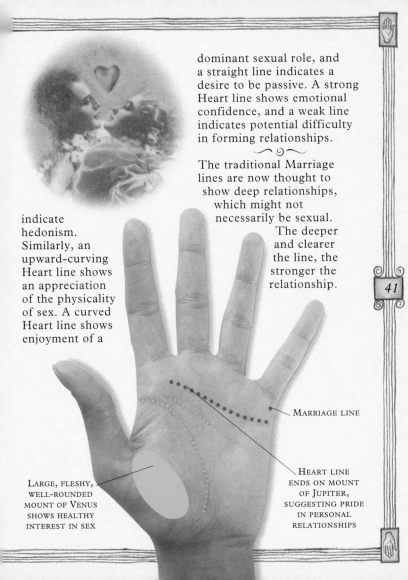

dominant sexual role, and a straight line indicates a desire to be passive. A strong Heart line shows emotional confidence, and a weak line indicates potential difficulty in forming relationships.

～۹～

The traditional Marriage lines are now thought to show deep relationships, which might not necessarily be sexual. The deeper and clearer the line, the stronger the relationship.

indicate hedonism. Similarly, an upward-curving Heart line shows an appreciation of the physicality of sex. A curved Heart line shows enjoyment of a

MARRIAGE LINE

HEART LINE
ENDS ON MOUNT
OF JUPITER,
SUGGESTING PRIDE
IN PERSONAL
RELATIONSHIPS

LARGE, FLESHY,
WELL-ROUNDED
MOUNT OF VENUS
SHOWS HEALTHY
INTEREST IN SEX

CAREER & SUCCESS

YOUR HANDS CAN SHOW VARIOUS PERSONAL QUALITIES,
SUCH AS PRACTICALITY, DETERMINATION, AMBITION,
INDEPENDENCE, REBELLIOUSNESS, AND INITIATIVE.
THESE QUALITIES WILL AFFECT YOUR CHOICE OF
CAREER, SUCCESS, AND LEVEL OF CONTENTMENT.

Line markings do not force you into a certain career. The Writer's Fork is found on the hands of many writers, but some people with a Writer's Fork choose to express their creativity in a different way.

~ 9 ~

The mounts can indicate career direction. The mount of Jupiter shows leadership; therefore a Fate line that ends there indicates ambition. A Fate line ending on

the mount of Apollo indicates success in the arts, and a Fate ending on the mount of Mercury shows business prowess. A Fate line that branches to more than one mount shows that several options are available to you. A well-developed mount of

CURVED HEAD LINE

WRITER'S FORK

FATE LINE IS
FRAGMENTED
AT START ON
MOUNT OF LUNA

Mercury suggests a teaching career, and a well-developed mount of Luna indicates work in the helping professions.

~ᴑ~

A clear Apollo line can show a successful creative career, and a break in the Fate and Career lines might mean a major change of job.

~ᴑ~

Long fingers indicate a talent for meticulous work, and short fingers suggest the ability to make quick-thinking decisions.

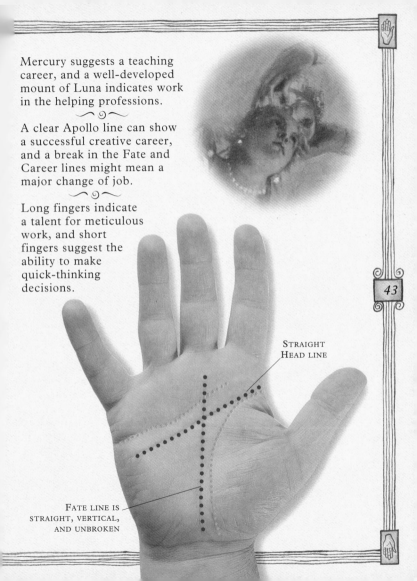

STRAIGHT
HEAD LINE

FATE LINE IS
STRAIGHT, VERTICAL,
AND UNBROKEN

HEALTH

THE COLOR AND TEXTURE OF YOUR HANDS, AND EVEN
THE LINES ON THE PALM, CAN INDICATE VULNERABLE
AREAS OF YOUR HEALTH. HOWEVER, ONE SINGLE
INDICATOR SHOULD NEVER BE TAKEN AS EVIDENCE OF
A POTENTIAL ILLNESS.

The Life line can be a
record of your health.
It can show a palmist that
you had an illness or accident
at a certain point in your life.
For example, childhood
respiratory problems often
show up as chaining near the
beginning of the Life line.
Crossbars across the Life line
can show an obstacle such as
an accident or illness.

Breaks or islands in the Head
line can indicate nervous
tension, mental problems, or

even physical injuries to the
head. Chaining and islands in
the Heart line might reveal
circulatory problems and
heart trouble. The color of

44

ISLAND ON
HEAD line
BENEATH
MIDDLE FINGER

ISLAND IN
MIDDLE OF
LIFE LINE

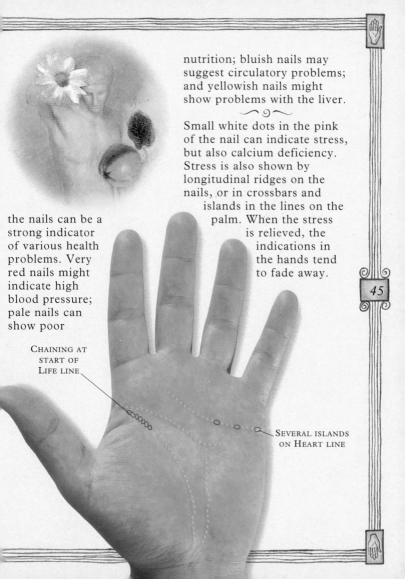

nutrition; bluish nails may suggest circulatory problems; and yellowish nails might show problems with the liver.

~⟨9⟩~

Small white dots in the pink of the nail can indicate stress, but also calcium deficiency. Stress is also shown by longitudinal ridges on the nails, or in crossbars and islands in the lines on the palm. When the stress is relieved, the indications in the hands tend to fade away.

the nails can be a strong indicator of various health problems. Very red nails might indicate high blood pressure; pale nails can show poor

CHAINING AT START OF LIFE line

SEVERAL ISLANDS ON HEART line

READING
THE PALMS

THE PALMIST IS INTERESTED IN THE WHOLE HAND, NOT
JUST THE LINES ON THE PALM. STRENGTH OF
CHARACTER, FOR EXAMPLE, CAN BE GAUGED FROM THE
HAND'S FIRMNESS AND FROM THE GRIP'S INTENSITY.

COCLES AND CHIROMANCY
*This engraving of the palmist Barthélemy
Coclès reading a palm is from a
16th-century book on chiromancy.*

When reading a palm, first examine the hand's shape. Compare the length of the fingers with the length of the palm to establish the personality type. Look at the mounts. Are they full or flat, firm or flabby? Skin texture and color, as well as nail condition, can be good indicators of overall health.

"Timing the lines" can be complicated. The Life line and Head line begin at the hand's edge between index finger and thumb, the Fate line starts near the wrist, and the Heart line begins at the hand's percussive edge. When "timing the lines," allow about $\frac{1}{16}$ in (1 mm) per year, but make the years 35–55 cover about $1\frac{1}{4}$ in (3 cm). The Fate line may start at various heights on the palm. To measure it, draw a vertical line from the top rascette to the crease at the middle finger's base and take the midpoint as 35. Some palmists take the midpoint of the Life line as 35, and work backward and forward from that point.

Always try to be sensitive when you are reading someone's palm. If you detect signs of serious illness, do not say, for example, that the person is likely to have a heart attack.

PAINTING PALMS
Michelangelo Caravaggio (1573–1610) is believed to have painted this picture of a palm reading, La Buona Ventura (The Fortune Teller), *around 1594.*

PALM READING 1

THE MOST NOTICEABLE FEATURE ABOUT THE RIGHT
HAND OF THIS 28-YEAR-OLD MAN IS THAT THE HEART
AND HEAD LINES ARE JOINED IN A SIMIAN LINE. THIS,
TOGETHER WITH OTHER LINES, INDICATES THE
COMPLEXITY OF HIS PERSONALITY.

The Simian line on
this man's right hand
indicates that it is always
difficult for him to make
decisions. His Head line
goes down; this shows that
he feels that he lacks
concentration,
which can make
him feel depressed.

However, he should have
more confidence in his very
good mind. His Girdle of
Venus is highly pronounced.
This suggests that he is a
perfectionist and can
be too rigid in his
control. This may
often appear as
intolerance.

GIRDLE OF
VENUS IS
PRONOUNCED

MYSTIC
CROSS

HEAD LINE
HAS SLIGHT
FORK

TOP RASCETTE
LOOPS UP,
SUGGESTING
CHILDHOOD
RESPONSIBILITY

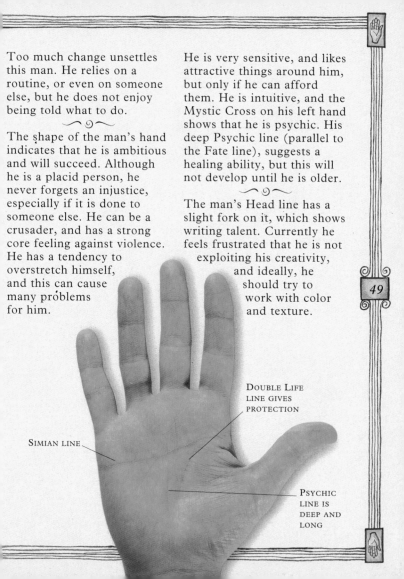

Too much change unsettles this man. He relies on a routine, or even on someone else, but he does not enjoy being told what to do.

~ ☙ ~

The shape of the man's hand indicates that he is ambitious and will succeed. Although he is a placid person, he never forgets an injustice, especially if it is done to someone else. He can be a crusader, and has a strong core feeling against violence. He has a tendency to overstretch himself, and this can cause many problems for him.

He is very sensitive, and likes attractive things around him, but only if he can afford them. He is intuitive, and the Mystic Cross on his left hand shows that he is psychic. His deep Psychic line (parallel to the Fate line), suggests a healing ability, but this will not develop until he is older.

~ ☙ ~

The man's Head line has a slight fork on it, which shows writing talent. Currently he feels frustrated that he is not exploiting his creativity, and ideally, he should try to work with color and texture.

DOUBLE LIFE LINE GIVES PROTECTION

SIMIAN LINE

PSYCHIC LINE IS DEEP AND LONG

PALM READING 2

THE HANDS OF THIS 33-YEAR-OLD WOMAN SHOW THAT
SHE HAS A TENDENCY TO OVERBURDEN HERSELF – THE
PALMIST SUGGESTS THAT IT WOULD BE BENEFICIAL
FOR HER HEALTH TO TAKE CONSIDERABLY MORE TIME
FOR REST AND RELAXATION.

This woman's long, continuous Head line suggests that she takes on too much responsibility for other people. As a result, she tends to get headaches through overtiredness. She is very sensible and needs to feel stable. When she gets tired, she simply must rest; this is shown by the breaks in her Heart line.

Whorls on the mound of the woman's index finger suggest that she should take care of her blood pressure as she

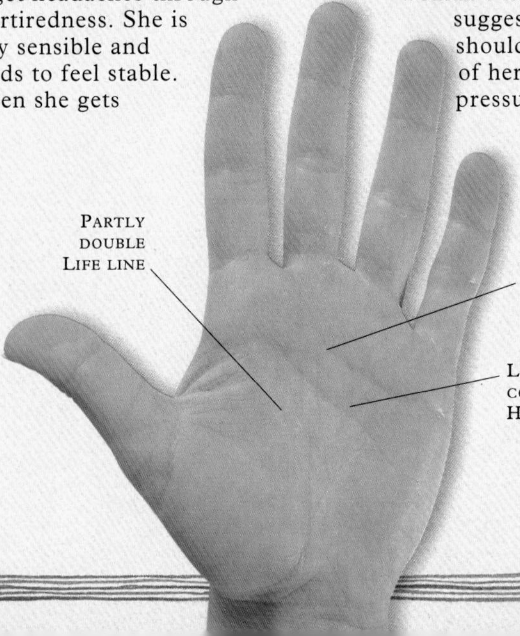

PARTLY
DOUBLE
LIFE line

BREAKS IN
HEART line

LONG,
CONTINUOUS
HEAD line

gets older. Outwardly, she may seem calm, but inwardly she can seethe, particularly if she is being coerced.

~ ☉ ~

The woman has a philosophical attitude, and a partly double Life line shows that she has considerable protection when she needs it. The break line between the Head line and the Life line shows that she has moved away from close family ties.

~ ☉ ~

In emotional relationships she is passionate and loyal, and her future relationships are more likely to be in the form of warm friendships than high sexual drama.

~ ☉ ~

The woman has ridges on all her fingers except her index finger, which shows that although she enjoys having beautiful objects around her, they are never essential.

~ ☉ ~

The creative aspect of the lines up to the point between her little and ring fingers cross over lines linked with children. This suggests that she would be most fulfilled by creating something suitable for children.

HIGHLY DEVELOPED MOUNT OF LUNA INDICATES CLAIRVOYANCY AND PSYCHIC ABILITY

BREAK LINE BETWEEN HEAD LINE AND LIFE LINE

TINY CROSSES ON FATE LINE SHOW HARD WORK FOR MONEY EARNED

PALM READING 3

THIS 39-YEAR-OLD MAN'S HANDS GIVE INFORMATION ABOUT HIS PERSONAL TENSIONS, RELATIONSHIPS, AND EMOTIONAL NEEDS AND PROBLEMS. HE TENDS TO REPRESS HIS FEELINGS, BUT IT WOULD BE MUCH MORE BENEFICIAL FOR HIM IF HE EXPRESSED THEM.

By taking all the indications of the lines together, it appears that this man has made himself tougher and stronger as he has developed. When he was young, he was very tolerant. However, he used to feel that people were taking advantage of him, and has consequently become more resolute.

~ ๑ ~

He is a perfectionist, and has creative ability that should be expressed. Although he fits in well with the crowd, he lacks

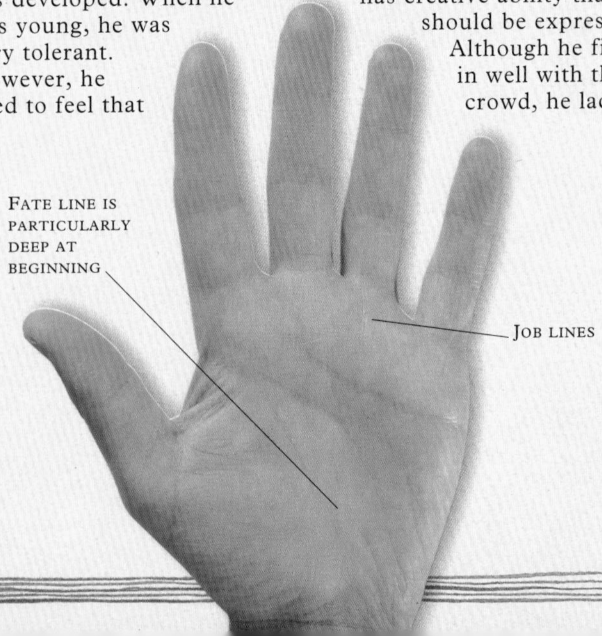

FATE LINE IS PARTICULARLY DEEP AT BEGINNING

JOB LINES

self-confidence. It takes him a long time to make friends, but they will then be his friends for life. He can sometimes be oversensitive to other people's feelings.

~ 0 ~

The man's Heart line is very chained, and has many islands. This suggests that his emotional relationships tend to be difficult and tempestuous. The several lines going down from the Heart line indicate that the other person usually breaks off the relationship, and show the hurt that he has felt from these rejections.

His Relationship or Marriage lines, at the percussive edge of the palm just below the little finger, show that a 13-year-old relationship with someone he worked with has now ended. His Career line curves down and links with the Relationship line, which shows that he was hurt by the ending of the relationship.

~ 0 ~

There are many crosses between the man's Head and Heart lines. This suggests that if his emotional life is upset, his work and everything else in his life suffers, too.

53

MANY ISLANDS ON HEART line

CHAINING ON LIFE line

CROSSES BETWEEN HEAD AND HEART LINES

PALM READING 4

THIS 35-YEAR-OLD WOMAN HAS A TENSE RESTLESSNESS IN HER HAND, SHOWN BY THE CROWDING TOGETHER OF THE LINES IN THE HOLLOW OF HER PALM. HER RESTLESSNESS IS LIKELY TO FORCE HER TO MOVE ON FROM HER PRESENT WAY OF LIFE.

During her childhood, the woman was extremely independent. She is very emotional, and has a strong sense of self and personal direction. This is shown by comparing the Fate line on the two hands. On the left hand (her passive hand, because she is right-handed) there is a very thin line showing, which indicates that she always wanted to be independent. Her right hand has an almost double Fate line, which shows a strong sense of self, coming from the mind. The

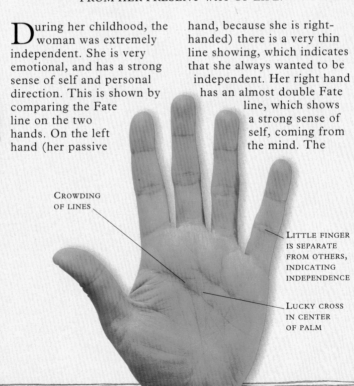

CROWDING
OF LINES

LITTLE FINGER
IS SEPARATE
FROM OTHERS,
INDICATING
INDEPENDENCE

LUCKY CROSS
IN CENTER
OF PALM

differences between the two hands show that her parents were far more cautious than she. She has reacted against their caution in her own life. The lines across the Life line towards the Fate line suggest that she loves taking risks and living dangerously.

~ ☉ ~

The woman is determined and a perfectionist, but she and other people cannot live up to her high ideals. This can create problems in her emotional relationships; they tend to be fiery, and then come to a halt.

Although she is working in a sphere that suits her, she is discontented with life. This is shown by the many breaks that come across her Fate line. She has a great urge to uproot herself. She will always be restless until she makes this move, and the move is inevitable because she feels compelled to make it. This is shown by comparing her Heart line and Life line, which come to one point. Her restlessness is building up to this point, when her great wanderlust will finally force her to move on.

55

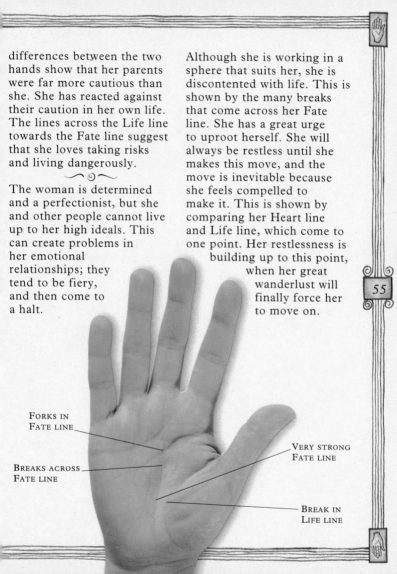

FORKS IN FATE LINE

BREAKS ACROSS FATE LINE

VERY STRONG FATE LINE

BREAK IN LIFE LINE

PALM READING 5

THE HANDS OF THIS 35-YEAR-OLD MAN SHOW THAT HE LACKS CONFIDENCE IN HIS OWN ABILITIES AND ALWAYS STRIVES TO DO BETTER. THE FIRM TEXTURE AND PHYSICAL STRENGTH OF HIS HANDS SUGGEST AN INTEREST IN SPORTS OR POSSIBLY SCULPTURE.

The deep lines on the man's palms suggest that he is attracted to the large and demanding rather than the insignificant. He has very high personal standards – although he meets them most of the time, he should be more prepared to relax them occasionally. He has a false self-image. Because of a general lack of encouragement when he was at school, he worries that he lacks substance, and consequently drives himself very hard.

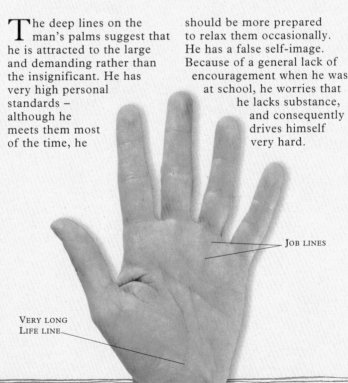

JOB LINES

VERY LONG LIFE LINE

The height of the man's ring finger compared to the height of his little finger indicates that he has musical ability. He is also artistically gifted, and he considers these gifts too important to compromise. His raised mounts, which usually point towards sensitivity and beauty, are extremely high. This indicates that sensitivity and beauty are dominant features in his life, and that he is sure of the standard that he wants to reach.

His Life line is very long, and part of it is

double. This means he has considerable protection in life if he needs it. The two very clear Job lines below his ring finger show that he is fortunate, because there are two jobs that he can do equally well.

The man's grip on the palmist's fingers is equal in each hand. This indicates that he is lucky in his work, because he can express his creative ability fully. He has teaching ability, and could easily train and help other people in creative work.

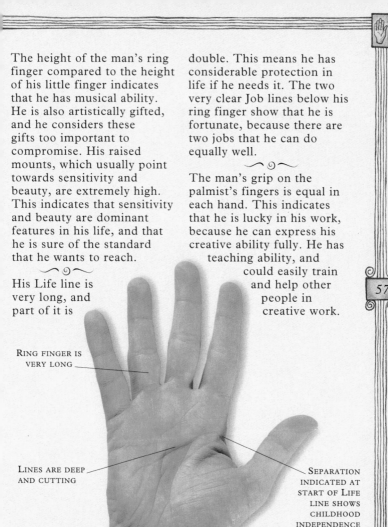

RING FINGER IS
VERY LONG

LINES ARE DEEP
AND CUTTING

SEPARATION
INDICATED AT
START OF LIFE
LINE SHOWS
CHILDHOOD
INDEPENDENCE

PALM READING 6

THE HANDS OF THIS 29-YEAR-OLD WOMAN REVEAL THE
SORT OF PERSON SHE IS, BUT ALSO HOW SHE RELATES
TO OTHER PEOPLE, INCLUDING HER PARTNER.
INFORMATION ABOUT HER PARTNER AND THEIR
RELATIONSHIP IS ALSO APPARENT IN HER PALMS.

The many fine lines on the woman's mount of Venus indicate that she is sensitive to what other people are thinking. She prefers to fit in with a crowd, and other people always enjoy her company.

She is a good mediator; she can see both sides of an issue, and other people will happily listen to her advice. Although people find it easy to talk to her, she has difficulty discussing important matters with other people.

RAISED FINGERTIPS SUGGEST LOVE OF BEAUTY, COUNTRYSIDE, AND PLANTS

LITTLE FINGER SLANTS INWARD

VERTICAL LINES UNDER MIDDLE FINGER AND RING FINGER

RIDGE IN TOP RASCETTE IMPLIES CHILDHOOD RESPONSIBILITY

By comparing the lines on her two hands, it is evident that she has made herself far more tolerant and open-minded than the way she was brought up. She has an excellent brain, but has a tendency to be distracted as things catch her interest.

~ ۞ ~

The woman is experiencing difficulty with her level of concentration. The islands on her Head line indicate that she has overburdened herself in too many areas of her life, but this should improve as she gets older.

"Timing the lines" suggests that she began her present emotional relationship around the age of 27. This relationship seems very strong. Her partner is about two years older than she is, which provides her with stability, shown by crosses below the index finger. Her little finger slants inward, indicating that she enjoys being seen as a couple.

~ ۞ ~

The two vertical lines under the middle and ring fingers show that she has a creative imagination and acting ability.

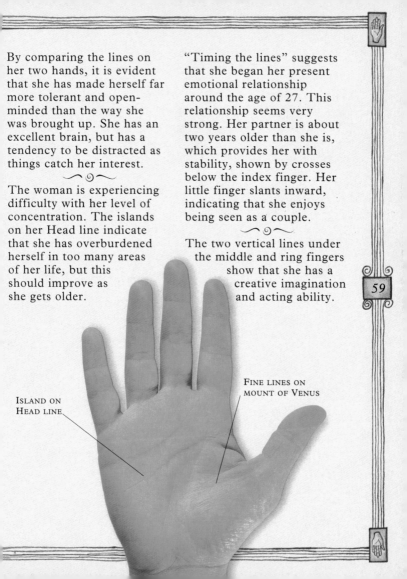

FINE LINES ON MOUNT OF VENUS

ISLAND ON HEAD LINE

INDEX

ACKNOWLEDGMENTS

Artworks
Gillie Newman 16, 17, 19, 20, 21, 22, 23, 25, 27;
Pelican Graphics 28, 29, 30, 31, 32, 33, 34,
35, 36, 37, 38, 39, 40, 41, 42, 43, 44, 45;
Sarah Perkins 4, 5, 7, 18, 19;
Anna Benjamin.

Special Photography
Steve Gorton

Editorial assistance Martha Swift,
Picture research Becky Halls and Ingrid Nilsson,
DTP design assistance Daniel McCarthy.

Hand Models
Angie Adams, Anna Benjamin, Derek Coombes,
Ursula Dawson, Jill Fornary, Candida Frith-Macdonald,
Sarah Goodwin, Steve Gorton, Lee Griffiths, Phil Hunt,
Cressida Joyce, Sharon Lucas, Tim Ridley, Kevin Ryan,
Tim Scott, Martha Swift, Alison Verity, Tracey Williams.
Thanks to Tamara at Mysteries for the palm readings.

Picture Credits

Key: *t* top; *c* center; *b* below; *l* left; *r* right

Bridgeman Art Library/Pinacoteca Capitolina,
Palazzo Conservatori, Rome,
The Fortune Teller, Michaelangelo Caravaggio 47*b*;
Images Color Library 10*bl*, 11*t*, 46*l*;
Mary Evans Picture Library 8*bl*, 9*tr*.